The Midwest

Amanda Jackson Green

Consultant

Brian Allman
Principal
Upshur County Schools, West Virginia

Publishing Credits

Rachelle Cracchiolo, M.S.Ed., *Publisher*
Emily R. Smith, M.A.Ed., *SVP of Content Development*
Véronique Bos, *VP of Creative*
Dona Herweck Rice, *Senior Content Manager*
Dani Neiley, *Editor*
Fabiola Sepulveda, *Series Graphic Designer*

Image Credits: p5 Marco Antonio Torres/Flickr; p8 © Iberfoto/Bridgeman Images; p10 Everett Collection/Bridgeman Images; p11 (top) The Stapleton Collection/Bridgeman Images; p11 (bottom) Courtesy of the Nebraska State Historical Society Photograph Collections; p12 © Art Gallery of Ontario/Bridgeman Images; p13 (top) Library of Congress [LC-DIG-pga-07508]; pp14-15 Everett Collection/Bridgeman Images; p16 Library of Congress [2009581130]; p17 Bridgeman Images; p18 Library of Congress [LC-USZC2-6148]; p19 Library of Congress [LC-USZ62-31238]; p21 (top) Chuck Kennedy/MCT/Newscom; p21 (bottom) Dennis Van Tine/ZUMAPRESS/Newscom; p25 (top) Wikimedia; p25 (bottom) GlowImages/Alamy Stock Photo; all other images from iStock and/or Shutterstock

Library of Congress Cataloging-in-Publication Data

Names: Green, Amanda Jackson, 1988- author.
Title: The Midwest / Amanda Jackson Green.
Description: Huntington Beach, CA : Teacher Created Materials, [2023] | Includes index. | Audience: Grades 4-6 | Summary: "The Midwest is one of the core regions of the United States. From the Great Lakes to the Great Plains, the Midwest is known for wide-open fields and friendly folks. Twelve states make up the Midwest. Each has its own government, people, and customs. Together, they have a big impact on the ways the rest of America eats, thinks, and lives"-- Provided by publisher.
Identifiers: LCCN 2022021239 (print) | LCCN 2022021240 (ebook) | ISBN 9781087691022 (paperback) | ISBN 9781087691183 (ebook)
Subjects: LCSH: Middle West--Juvenile literature.
Classification: LCC F351 .G773 2023 (print) | LCC F351 (ebook) | DDC 977--dc23/eng/20220504
LC record available at https://lccn.loc.gov/2022021239
LC ebook record available at https://lccn.loc.gov/2022021240

Shown on the cover is a farm in Iowa.

TCM | Teacher Created Materials

5482 Argosy Avenue
Huntington Beach, CA 92649
www.tcmpub.com

ISBN 978-1-0876-9102-2

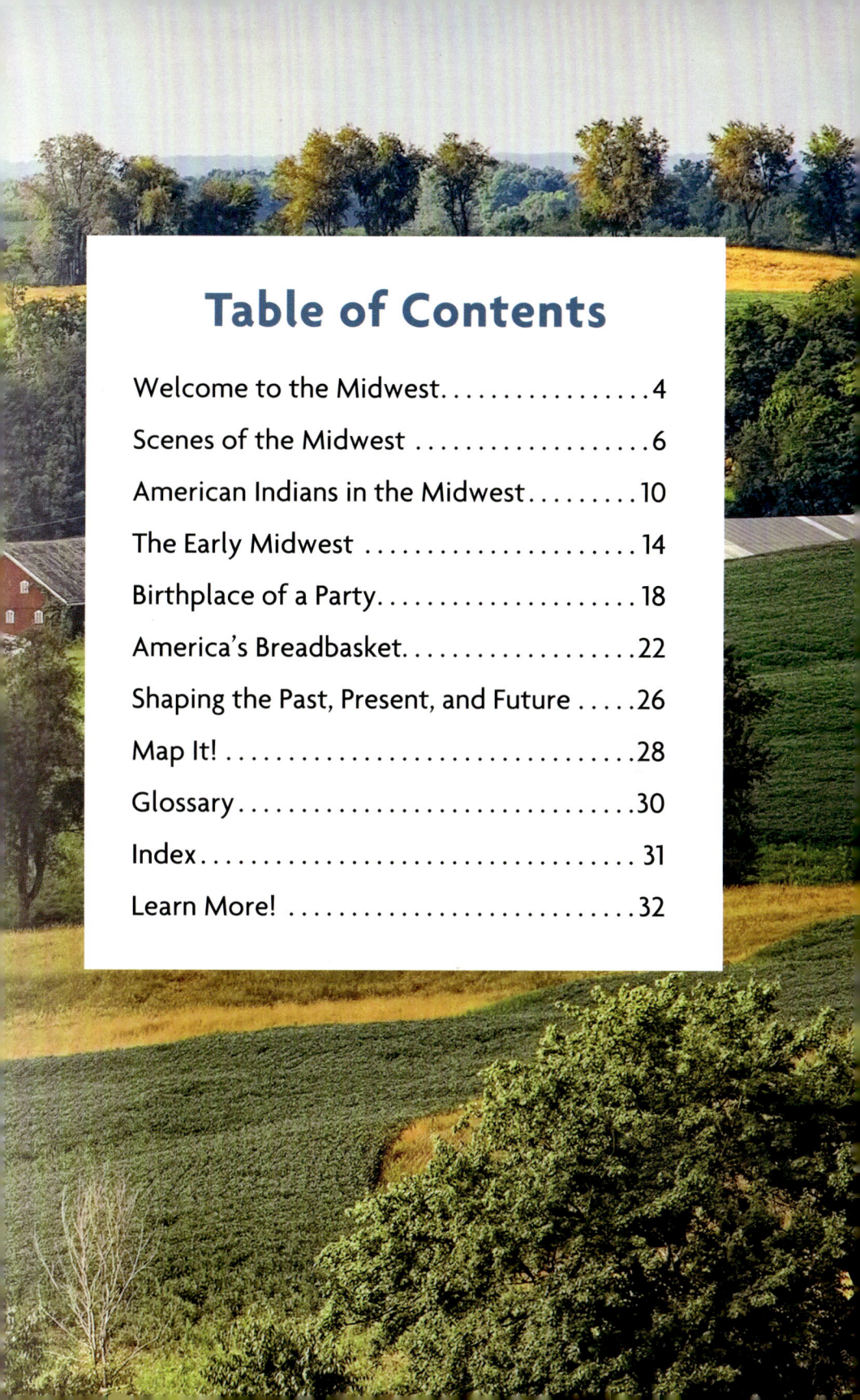

Table of Contents

Welcome to the Midwest. 4

Scenes of the Midwest 6

American Indians in the Midwest 10

The Early Midwest 14

Birthplace of a Party. 18

America's Breadbasket. 22

Shaping the Past, Present, and Future 26

Map It! 28

Glossary. 30

Index. 31

Learn More! 32

Welcome to the Midwest

The Midwest is an important **region** of the United States. It is made up of 12 states. To the north are Minnesota, Wisconsin, Michigan, and North Dakota. Kansas, Missouri, Illinois, Indiana, and Ohio make up the southern part of the region. South Dakota and Nebraska frame the west. Iowa sits right in the middle. Two mountain ranges flank the Midwest. The Rocky Mountains stand tall to the west. To the east are the Appalachians. The Great Lakes mark the northern edge.

One in five Americans call the Midwest home. Still, residents are fairly spread out. If everyone living in the Midwest divided up their land, and everyone living in New York City did the same, they would see a big difference. The land 1 person in the Midwest got would equal about the same as the land 300 people shared in New York City.

UNITED STATES MIDWEST

States in the Midwest are considered to be in "America's Heartland." The area is known for its wide-open spaces and friendly people. Small towns and big cities are filled with diverse ways of life. Visitors come from far and wide to enjoy the region's sites, too. Others depend on Midwesterners for food, goods, and big ideas. In some ways, what happens in the Midwest affects the entire world.

Population: 1

The Midwest features one of America's biggest cities and one of its smallest towns. Chicago, Illinois, is the country's third-largest city. More than 2.5 million people live there. Monowi, Nebraska, has only one resident—Ms. Elsie Eiler.

Scenes of the Midwest

The Midwest landscape is mostly flat. Much of the region overlaps with the Great Plains. The land is made up of high **plateaus** and vast expanses of land. Native plants include woody shrubs, such as sagebrush. There are also many wildflowers and different types of grasses as well. With plenty of plants, the Great Plains are an ideal spot for grazing animals, such as cattle and bison. Pronghorns, prairie dogs, coyotes, and more call it home.

Heading east, the plains give way to rolling hills and peaks. The Black Hills of South Dakota are made of granite. The rugged terrain is dotted with pine trees and other evergreens. Black Elk Peak is the range's highest point. It is 7,242 feet (2,207 meters) tall!

Badlands National Park,
South Dakota

Mako Sica

Badlands National Park offers views of ancient cliffs, rocks, and fossils. The area gets its name from the Lakota people. For hundreds of years, they have called it *mako sica*. This translates to "bad lands."

Lake Superior, Michigan

Lakes and Rivers

Water has played an important role in the lives of people in the Midwest for centuries. Half of the states in the Midwest rest along the edges of the Great Lakes. Lake Superior, Lake Michigan, Lake Huron, Lake Erie, and Lake Ontario make up this chain of lakes. Spanning more than 750 miles (1,207 kilometers) from east to west, it is the largest body of fresh water in the world.

fishing in Lake Michigan

Cincinnati and the Cincinnati River

Throughout history, Midwesterners have relied on the Great Lakes for food, travel, and sport. The lakes support major cities such as Cleveland, Ohio, and Chicago, Illinois. The Mississippi, Missouri, and Ohio rivers also support commerce and daily life in the Midwest. Boats move people and goods along the waterways. Rivers also serve as a source of drinking water for nearby towns and cities.

Climate

The Midwest has a humid **continental climate**. Rainfall is steady across every season. The weather changes a lot from season to season. Summer days are often very hot and sunny. A lack of trees can make it hard to find shade. Winter brings freezing weather. Lakes and ponds turn to ice, and snow covers the ground.

Severe weather is common. Cool air moves in from the north. Warm air rises from the south. The currents collide over the flatlands. **Tornadoes** and thunderstorms form as a result. In 2020, Illinois had over 70 tornadoes. It is no wonder people call parts of this region Tornado Alley! High winds can damage buildings. Flying objects are a danger to people and animals. In some cities, loud sirens warn people to find shelter.

Wild Winds

Tornadoes form a column of swirling air. These twisters can move as fast as 300 miles (about 483 kilometers) per hour. The resulting winds are strong enough to rip the roofs off houses and lift cars off the ground!

American Indians in the Midwest

American Indians have lived in the Midwest region since before recorded history. Long ago, there were two main tribal nations in the area. These were the Great Lakes and the Great Plains groups. Each group had its own unique culture. The people of the tribes also had a wide range of languages and beliefs. They did have some things in common, though. Most people were hunters and gatherers. Fishing was important in many tribes because of the abundance of water in the Midwest.

Great Lakes Tribes

As early as the 16th century, tribes constructed villages on the banks of the Great Lakes. Among them were the Ottawa and Huron tribes. Great Lakes tribes relied on the lakes' plants and wildlife for food. The people used canoes to float on the water while fishing. The wigwam was a common dwelling in Great Lakes villages. Tribal members used tree bark and saplings to build domes for their homes. Grasses were packed into the walls to keep out cold air. At the centers of the wigwams were firepits. The firepits served as heaters while residents slept inside.

painting of American Indians on ice, 1858

daily life inside a wigwam

Doctor for Her People

Susan La Flesche Picotte was part of the Omaha tribe. In 1889, she earned a degree in medicine. She was the first American Indian to do so. In 1913, she opened the first private hospital on a reservation.

Great Plains Indians

Farther south, the people of dozens of American Indian tribes lived in the Great Plains. The Cheyenne and Blackfoot peoples are part of this group. Great Plains Indians often lived in special dwellings called tepees. People used long, wooden poles to form a tepee's frame. The poles were tied together at the top and spread out at the bottom. The outside of the dwelling was wrapped with a large covering, usually made from bison hide.

Tepees were well-suited to the lifestyle of the Great Plains Indians. They hunted bison for food. The animals' hides and bones were used to make everyday objects such as clothes, blankets, and tools. Tribes had to move often to follow the **migration** of herds. Tepees were lightweight and easy to carry for the journey. When the people arrived at a new destination, they could quickly rebuild their homes.

tepees

Some Great Plains tribes were more **sedentary**. This includes the Osage and Pawnee peoples. They settled in one place for longer periods. Earth lodges were a common type of shelter among them. Along with hunting, the people of these tribes farmed crops such as maize, beans, and squash. But farming in the Great Plains was not easy to do. Drought was common. Many of the people used rituals in hopes of bringing rain or sunshine.

The American Bison

Bison are the largest mammals in North America. Herds of these massive beasts once roamed the Great Plains. American Indian tribes relied on them for survival. They hunted the bison for food. They also used the thick, shaggy hides for clothing and shelter.

The Early Midwest

French settlers arrived in the Great Lakes area during the 1500s. **Missionaries** aimed to convert local tribes to their religions. Others came in search of silver and gold. Instead, they found another valuable resource: animal furs.

Fur was a popular **textile** in France. It was used to make clothes and hats. Beaver fur was in high demand. It was rarely found in Europe. But beavers were bountiful in the Midwest. French settlers often traded with local tribes. They offered guns, metal tools, and other items in exchange for furs. They transported the furs back to France. There, merchants sold the furs for a major profit.

Parlez-vous français?

Many Midwest cities take their names from the French language. One example is the former missionary town of Des Moines, Iowa. The origin of its name is controversial. It could have come from *de moyen*. This is French for "in the middle." It also could have come from the French phrase for "the place of the monks."

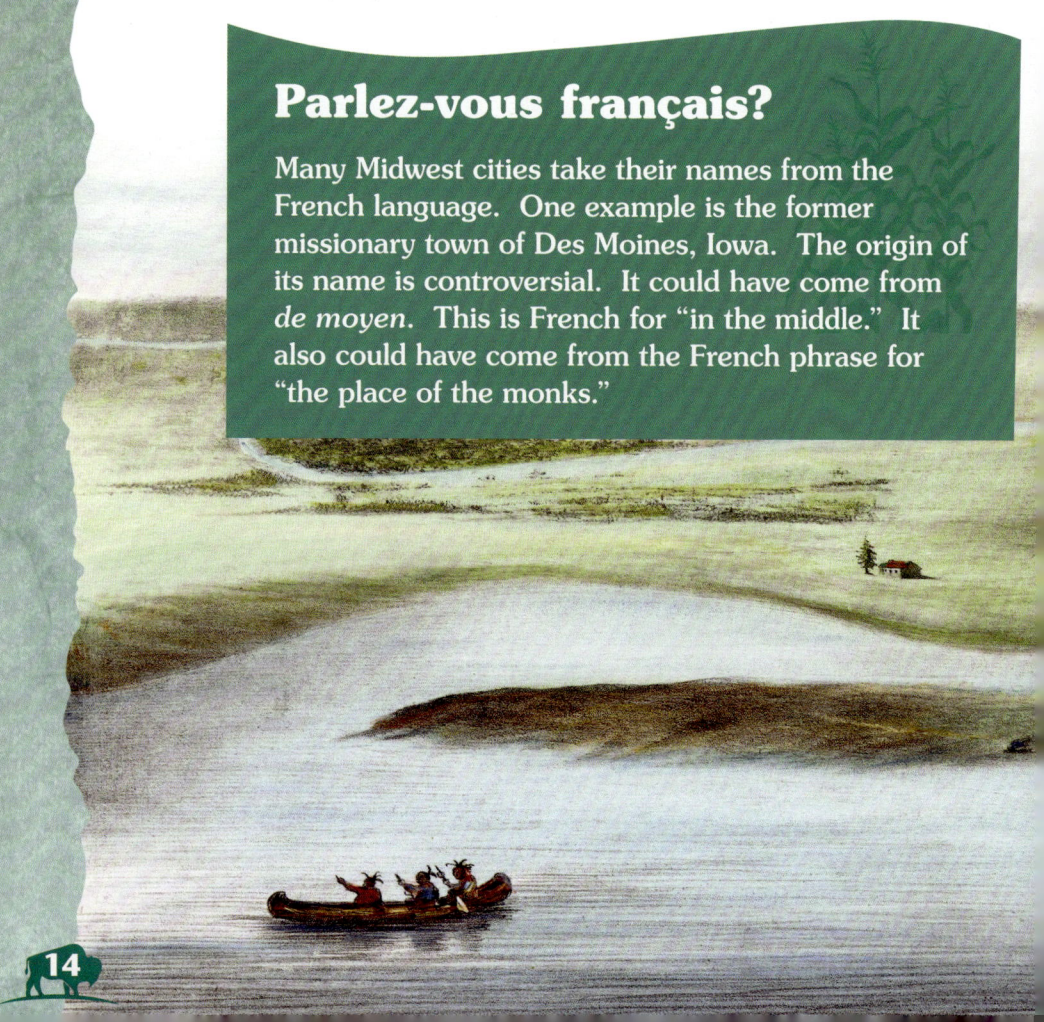

In the 18th century, British colonists entered the Midwest. The newcomers fought the French for rights to the land. Some American Indian tribes **allied** with the French. Others joined the British side. A series of wars followed. In the end, the parties came to a peace **treaty**. In the Treaty of Paris, Britain gave up all claims to the area.

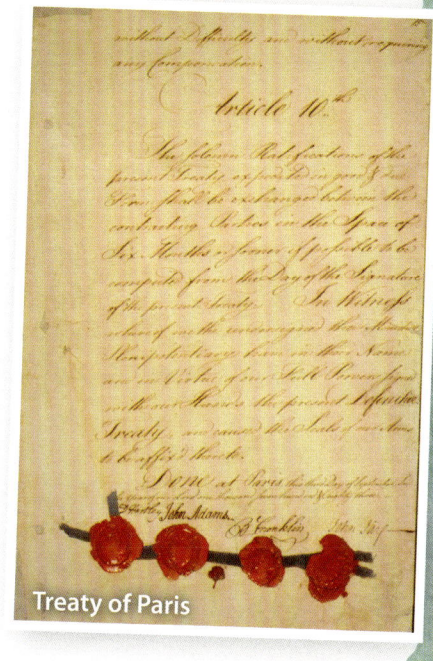

Treaty of Paris

By the early 1800s, France had control of the Midwest region, and British colonists had won independence. The colonists formed their own nation: the United States of America. As the country grew, its citizens began to migrate westward in search of new lands to settle.

Chicago, 1820

During French rule, the Midwest was part of a bigger region. The area was called the Louisiana Territory. It spanned 828,000 square miles (about 2.1 million square kilometers). In 1803, U.S. leaders made a deal with France. The young nation bought the Louisiana Territory. The price was 15 million dollars. That may seem like a lot of money. But it added up to only about three cents per acre! The Louisiana Purchase doubled the size of the United States. Over time, the land would be split into 15 states. Some of them would make up the Midwest.

Westward Expansion

During the next few decades, Americans moved west in high numbers. The government even offered free plots of land to citizens. In return, settlers agreed to build homes and tend the land. **Immigrants** also settled in the new area. They came from countries such as Germany, Ireland, and Russia. After the Civil War, formerly enslaved Black people headed west to start new lives. The Midwest became home to people from many walks of life.

LOUISIANA PURCHASE, 1803. FLORIDA PURCHASE, 1819.

Americans believed they had a right to all land in the west. That included the homes of American Indian tribes. The U.S. government forced the people of the tribes onto reservations in the region's upper states. Many descendants of the **displaced** people still live there.

covered wagons along the Oregon Trail

The Oregon Trail

Many settlers who traveled west did so on the Oregon Trail. The road began in Missouri. It stretched west to Oregon. Covered wagons pulled by oxen were the main vehicles among travelers. The journey took about five months to complete.

Birthplace of a Party

As is true of most regions in the United States, people in the Midwest take part in a number of **civic** activities and duties. Voters select leaders at each level of government. Local governments take care of programs such as public safety, schools, and parks. State governments manage roads, state courts, and other systems. Residents pay **taxes** to support these programs. Some taxes are based on income. Others are assessed on the value of property. Sales tax comes from fees added to the cost of goods and services.

Peanuts of the Midwest

Charles Schultz created the *Peanuts* comic strip. His famous characters include Charlie Brown and Snoopy. Schultz was born in Minneapolis, Minnesota, and his Peanuts world is based on his own childhood. Many people assume that Charlie Brown and the gang live in the Midwest.

This schoolhouse is where people think the Republican Party was founded.

Since its early days, the Midwest region has played a major role in U.S. **politics**. In 1854, about 30 settlers gathered in Ripon, Wisconsin. The group called for an end to slavery in the West. They felt that their leaders were not doing enough to push for change. They decided to form their own group. It became the Republican Party. This party has changed through time but remains one of the leading parties in the nation.

Many leaders also got their start in America's Heartland. In fact, one-fourth of U.S. presidents were born in one of the region's twelve states. Seven were born in Ohio alone.

OHIO

Iowa Is First

There are two main political parties in the United States. One is the Republican Party. The Democratic Party is the other. Most people who run for president do so with the support of one of these parties. Each party chooses a candidate based on how many votes they receive in the **primary election**. The primary is the contest by which parties choose a nominee. It begins at the state level.

The Midwest plays an important role in this process. This is, in most part, because of Iowa. Iowa is traditionally the first state to hold its primary election. In Iowa, the contest is done by **caucus**. Each party hosts its own caucus. These gatherings are held in school gyms, churches, and even homes. During the meetings, members try to convince one another to vote for a certain person. They give speeches and hold debates. At the end, members vote publicly. The candidate with the most votes for their party receives the party's nomination.

It is often believed that winning Iowa's support helps one's chances of winning in other states. As such, some candidates begin their campaigns in the Hawkeye state.

IOWA

The Iowa State Fair

The Iowa State Fair is a yearly event. It takes place in Des Moines, Iowa. Attendees enjoy games, contests, and special foods. Candidates for president often attend the event. They meet voters. They also give speeches about why people should vote for them.

President Barack Obama

Senator Mitt Romney

America's Breadbasket

The Midwest is one of the most important farming areas in the United States. Warm summers and fertile soil make the Midwest perfect for farming. In the areas with low rainfall, farmers use **irrigation** to water their crops. They pump water from rivers, lakes, and wells. Then, they move it to the fields through canals or pipes.

Fields of crops cover about 127 million acres (51 million hectares) of the Midwest. These farmlands can be split into three main areas, or belts. Kansas and Nebraska are in the southern part of the Wheat Belt. In the north are North Dakota, South Dakota, and Minnesota. Wheat is the main crop in these states. After harvesting, the grain is used to make flour, bread, and cereals. This is where the Midwest gets the nickname "America's Breadbasket."

The second farming region is the Corn Belt. It covers Illinois, Iowa, and Missouri. Parts of Nebraska, Indiana, and Kansas are also included. Corn and soybeans grow bountifully in the area's rainy climate. Corn syrup, cooking oils, and tofu are just a few of the products made from these crops.

harvesting machine in a wheat field

farm in Illinois

How Big Is an Acre?

The size of a farm or other plot of land is often measured by acres. An acre is the size of about two soccer fields. One acre is equal to 4,840 square yards (about 4,047 square meters).

Minnesota, Wisconsin, and Michigan make up the Dairy Belt. These states have cooler summers and freezing winters. Not many crops can survive that climate. However, tall grasses thrive. These grasses are used to make hay to feed cattle. Some cows are raised and sold for meat. Others produce milk. The milk is used to make cheese, ice cream, and other dairy products.

A Nuts-and-Bolts Economy

Factories and food plants are large sources of money in the Midwest. Many residents depend on these businesses for jobs. Factory workers make and build all kinds of **exports**. Your family car, refrigerator, or computer may have been made in the Midwest. Midwest factories also produce much of America's capital goods. These are products, such as tools and machines, that are used to make other products.

Visitors Welcome

The Midwest offers lots of things for visitors to see and do. One example is the Willis Tower in Chicago, Illinois. The tower offers amazing views of the city. Indiana hosts one of the world's biggest car races. It is called the Indy 500. The race brings hundreds of thousands of visitors each year. Tourists spend money on lodging and food. They also buy other goods and services. All of these things support the Midwest's economy.

Willis Tower, Chicago

Motor City

Detroit, Michigan, is known as a center of the auto industry. It was there that Henry Ford founded the Ford Motor Company in 1903. Since then, car companies have provided thousands of Detroit workers with jobs. No wonder it is called Motor City!

workers at the Ford Motor Company, 1913

GMC Truck Plant, Michigan, 2021

Shaping the Past, Present, and Future

The Midwest region of the United States is a land of flat prairies and rolling hills. It is made up of 12 states. Each state has its own unique customs, people, and government. But they combine to make up one of America's most important regions.

For hundreds of years, people have been drawn to the Midwest. American Indians made use of the area's wide range of plants and wildlife. Colonists moved west for the promise of good soil and other resources. Hopeful immigrants found freedom on the Great Lakes and the Great Plains. Each group brought with it diverse beliefs and ways of life. Together, they built a productive economy. It is one that feeds people across the nation and the world.

Duluth, Minnesota

factory work, Indiana

The Midwest's reach goes far beyond corn and wheat. Big ideas and major leaders have come from the region, too. From farmers to presidents, Midwesterners have a big impact on the rest of the United States. They have shaped America's past and present. They will continue to influence the country's future for decades to come.

corn harvest, Minnesota

Why the Midwest?

At one time, the region now called the West was known as the Far West. The area that came to be known as the Midwest was the region that fell between the Far West and the East. *Mid* means "between" or "in the middle."

Map It!

The Midwest is a major center for the U.S. economy. Farming is among the region's most important industries. On pages 22–24, you learned about the region's three main farming areas, or belts. These include the Wheat Belt, the Corn Belt, and the Dairy Belt. Create a map that identifies the states in each belt.

1. Start with a map of the Midwest or a map of the whole United States.
2. Select a different color for each belt. For example, you might choose red for the Wheat Belt, yellow for the Corn Belt, and blue for the Dairy Belt.
3. Color each state with the color that corresponds to its farming belt. Some states may be part of more than one belt. In this case, draw stripes across the state in the colors that go with each belt.
4. When you are finished coloring, take a look at your map. Think about these questions:

   ❖ Do you notice any patterns?

   ❖ What do the states in each belt have in common?

   ❖ Are they spread out or close to one another?

   ❖ Where are they in relation to bodies of water?

cows in rural Iowa

NORTH DAKOTA

Bismarck

MINNESOTA

Red Lake

Lake Superior

Duluth

Fargo

SOUTH DAKOTA

WISCONSIN

St Paul

Eau Claire

Minneapolis

Mississippi

Appleton

Lake Michigan

Lake Huron

Rapid City

Pierre

Rochester

Madison

Milwaukee

Grand Rapids

MICHIGAN

Detroit

Lansing

Lake Erie

Sioux Falls

IOWA

Chicago

Toledo

Cleve

Missouri

Rockford

NEBRASKA

Sioux City

Cedar Rapids

South Bend

Fort Wayne

Akron

Omaha

Des Moines

Davenport

ILLINOIS

Gary

INDIANA

Columbus

OHIO

VIR

Lincoln

Springfield

Indianapolis

Cincinnati

Ohio

Ch

Kansas City

St. Louis

Luisville

Frankfort

Topeka

Jefferson City

Lexington

do

KANSAS

Evansville

KENTUCKY

gs

Arkansas

MISSOURI

Wichita

Springfield

Nashville

Knoxville

Oklahoma City

ARKA

Glossary

allied—agreed to work together

caucus—a meeting of members of a political party for the purpose of choosing candidates for an election

civic—relating to being a citizen

continental climate—a climate with very hot summers and very cold winters

displaced—removed from an area, usually by force

exports—products that are sent to another state or country to be sold there

immigrants—people who come to a country to live there

irrigation—the method of supplying land with water by using artificial means (such as pipes)

migration—movement from one place to another at different times of year

missionaries—people who travel to a foreign country to do religious work

plateaus—large, flat areas of land that are higher than surrounding areas of land

politics—activities related to influencing the actions and policies of a government

primary election—a contest to select the candidates for a general election, especially for the role of president (in the United States)

region—a part of a country that is different or separate from other parts in some way

sedentary—staying or living in one place instead of moving to different places

taxes—amounts of money that governments require people to pay according to their incomes, the value of their properties, etc. and that is used to pay for things done by the government

textile—a fabric that is used to make clothing

tornadoes—violent and destructive storms in which powerful winds move around a central point

treaty—an official agreement that is made between two or more countries or groups

Index

America's Breadbasket, 22

Badlands National Park, 6

Blackfoot, 12

Black Hills, 6

Cheyenne, 12

Corn Belt, 22

Dairy Belt, 24

Democratic Party, 20

Ford, Henry, 25

Great Lakes, 4, 7–8, 10, 14, 26

Great Plains, 6, 10, 12–13, 26

Huron tribe, 10

Illinois, 4–5, 8, 22, 24

Indiana, 4, 22, 24, 27

Iowa State Fair, 20

Kansas, 4, 22

Louisiana Purchase, 16

Louisiana Territory, 16

Michigan, 4, 7, 24–25

Minnesota, 4, 18, 22, 24, 26–27

Missouri, 4, 8, 17, 22

North Dakota, 4, 22

Ohio, 4, 8, 19

Oregon Trail, 17

Ottawa tribe, 10

Picotte, Susan La Flesche, 11

Republican Party, 19–20

Wheat Belt, 22

Wisconsin, 4, 19, 24

farm fields north of Dubuque, Iowa

Learn More!

You have read about some of the famous people from the Midwest. Now, do some research on other well-known Midwesterners.

* Choose one person from one of the 12 Midwestern states, and research their life.

* Design a biography poster with details about their life.

* Include a picture of the person.

* Add some unique or interesting facts that set this person apart. You might include things they have accomplished, special talents, or popular quotes.

* Make sure to include which Midwestern state your subject called home.

Kansas harvesters unloading grain into a grain cart